Color Train

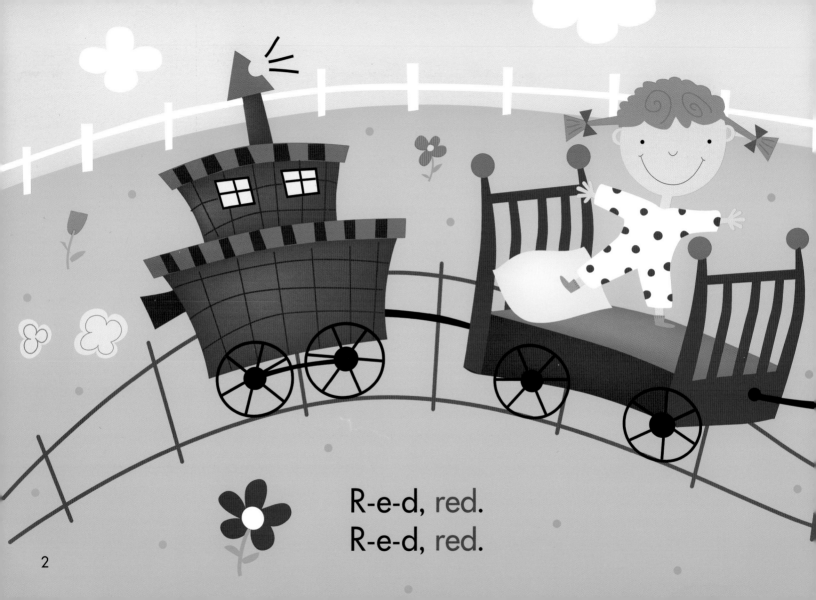

R-e-d, red.
R-e-d, red.

Red bird, red head,
red heart, red bed.
R-e-d, red.

3

B-l-u-e, blue.
B-l-u-e, blue.
Blue berries, blue eyes,
blue bird, blue sky.
B-l-u-e, blue.

Y-e-l-l-o-w, yellow.
Y-e-l-l-o-w, yellow.
Yellow flowers, yellow sun,
lemon pie, bananas, yum!
Y-e-l-l-o-w, yellow.

5

G-r-e-e-n, green.
G-r-e-e-n, green.
Green grass, green grapes,
cucumbers, lizards, snakes.
G-r-e-e-n, green.

6

P-u-r-p-l-e, purple.
P-u-r-p-l-e, purple.
Purple **balls**, purple **plums**,
purple **shirts**, purple **gum**.
P-u-r-p-l-e, purple.

O-r-a-n-g-e, orange.
O-r-a-n-g-e, orange.
Orange pumpkins, orange leaves,
orange juice, orange trees.
O-r-a-n-g-e, orange.

8

B-l-a-c-k, **black**.
B-l-a-c-k, **black**.
Black night, **black** cat,
black panther, **black** hat.
B-l-a-c-k, **black**.

Roar!

B-r-o-w-n, brown.
B-r-o-w-n, brown.
Brown cow, chocolate cake,
brown leaves, brown rake.
B-r-o-w-n, brown.

W-h-i-t-e, white.
W-h-i-t-e, white.
White cloud, white snow,
white rabbit, white bow.
W-h-i-t-e, white.

P-i-n-k, pink.
P-i-n-k, pink.
Pink ribbons, pink nose,
pink flamingo, pink rose.
P-i-n-k, pink.